Original title:
The Brooch's Gaze

Copyright © 2025 Creative Arts Management OÜ
All rights reserved.

Author: Tobias Sterling
ISBN HARDBACK: 978-1-80586-091-4
ISBN PAPERBACK: 978-1-80586-563-6

Gaze of the Adorned

On a coat made of fluff, with a shimmer so bright,
A little pin winks, full of mischief and light.
It peers at the sock, a neighbor so bold,
Whispers sweet jokes that are priceless, not sold.

With sequins that dance and a style unique,
It claims to be wise, though its words are quite cheek.
It giggles at necklines, the flair they bestow,
A council of bling, oh, what a fine show!

In the Shadow of the Ornament

Hiding in the folds of a jacket once grand,
A sparkly little thing, scheming by hand.
"Did you see that tie? So mismatched and wrong!"
It chuckles and jests, a mischief-filled song.

In the corner it peeks, on the lookout for fun,
A snicker at lapels, all outdone by one.
It barks at the buttons, so round and so loud,
While fashion's off guard, it feels oh so proud!

A Twinkle in the Fabric

There's a shimmer alive in the mix of the threads,
A twinkle that knows where the laughter is fed.
With a wink to the pocket and a nudge to the seam,
It sparks a hilarity, a wonderful dream.

"Why match shoes to jackets? It's all a charade!"
Chortles the glimmer, in colors displayed.
It tickles your fancy, this playful delight,
Wearing bold patterns, all day and all night!

The Hidden Eye Amongst the Finery

Nestled in jewels and a shimmer of lace,
A sly little glance having quite the embrace.
It winks at the necklace, a chain so austere,
And mocks the grand pearls that pretend to be dear.

Beneath the grand hat, it spies with a grin,
At socks full of stripes, oh, where do we begin?
It giggles with glee at the hats worn askew,
Celebrating quirks with a jest and two blue!

Elegance in Entropy

A shiny gem, it gave a wink,
It held secrets, don't you think?
On an ugly sweater, oh so grand,
It sparkled bright, just like a band.

What's that? A cousin's cat did play,
Chasing threads on grandma's day.
The gem's now lost, it rolled away,
While laughter echoed in dismay.

Symbols of the Past

A quirky pin from years ago,
Stuck on hats, it's quite the show!
With a smile, it waves at us,
Telling tales that surely fuss.

Next to grandpa, sharp and tall,
It lands in stew—a tragic fall!
But laughter rises from the mess,
A story told, we all confess.

Echoing Elegance

At fancy parties, it takes a seat,
On a dance floor, oh so neat.
It twirls and jigs; it knows no bounds,
A royal touch in silly sounds.

But here it sits, in grand display,
Next to the chips, it steals the play!
With every crinkle, every cheer,
Its elegance, we hold so dear.

A Dance of Precious Stones

With diamonds all around the room,
A disco ball? No! It's full bloom!
Gems make eyes roll and heads spin,
While folks beneath them laugh and grin.

So come, let's twist and shimmy tight,
A jester's jest, what a sight!
With jewels dancing like a song,
Who knew that folly could feel so strong?

Locket of Lost Moments

In a pocket, small and round,
A treasure lost, now seldom found.
It holds a grin, a wink, a jest,
Of awkward dates, we laughed the best.

A selfie snapped, my hair askew,
Now framed forever, just for you.
It squeaks with joy when tales unfold,
Of spilled drinks and truths retold.

The locket laughs at time's embrace,
A snapshot of a playful face.
Each memory twirls in silly dance,
Replaying our most clumsy chance.

Embers of Past Encounters

In the corner, smoky light,
Flickering memories ignite.
A whisper shared across the room,
Or how you tripped, oh what a boom!

Tales of dinners gone awry,
Spaghetti shirts, and sauce gone shy.
We chuckle through the tales we weave,
As ghostly embers bob and leave.

The ghosts of laughter line the walls,
Where awkward pauses grip the halls.
Each ember sparks a current blast,
Reviving smiles from our past.

Echoes in the Embellishments

Gold and glitter, shiny bright,
Dancing dolls in silly light.
An echo laughs from every stone,
A wink that whispers, you're not alone.

A bracelet clinks like feet in line,
Each charm a tale, a plot divine.
From frog-fitted hats to flapping wings,
The jests from life are the richest things.

Beads and baubles sing in glee,
Recalling moments wild and free.
In every twist, a giggle bounds,
The echoes live in veiled sounds.

The Pendant's Watchful Heart

A pendant swings on laughter's thread,
With tales of blunders often fed.
It peeks at faces, grins so wide,
As life's grand circus takes a ride.

It saw the fall, the flustered grin,
The moment when we'd all begin.
To dance on floors, so slick and slick,
A watchful heart of mischief quick.

It giggles soft through paths we tread,
Chasing dreams like crumbs of bread.
Each clattering step a merry twirl,
The pendant spins our jolly whirl.

Colorful Whispers of History

A pin with tales, it winks and grins,
Holding secrets of all our sins.
It rolls its eyes at the tales it knows,
Like a gossiping cat in a row of bows.

Its jewels sparkle with a cheeky flair,
As it mocks the days when no one would care.
With a poke and a jest, it plays its part,
In a storybook world, it's the quirky heart.

Memory Threaded in Gold

A charm that jingles with every laugh,
It nudges your memory—what a craft!
Reminding you of that awkward dance,
When you tripped and fell, seized by chance.

Each glimmer tells of friends and foes,
Of days so silly, they slip between toes.
With a wink and a twist, it keeps us aligned,
A golden thread in a world, unrefined.

Timeless Trinkets

In a drawer of wonders, it clinks and clatters,
Each sparkle a story, each shimmer that matters.
Poking fun at trends that come and go,
It dresses up memories, stealing the show.

Adorning the laughter of past little pranks,
It snickers quietly, filling in blanks.
With every twist of its colorful fate,
It teases the future and dances with fate.

Luminescence Unheard

A glimmer that never seeks to be seen,
It sparkles with mischief, where've you been?
Quietly chuckling at our clumsy ways,
It's the best witness to our goofy days.

It holds no grudges; it's here for the fun,
With every laugh, it glistens, it runs.
In the background, it twirls, a silent zany,
A treasure of joy, both cheeky and grainy.

Charmed by a Subtle Look

A glimmer caught the eye, so sly,
It winked as I strolled by, oh me, oh my!
"Look at me!" it seemed to shout,
With a twinkle that turned my frown about.

In a crowd, it stood with pride,
A tiny spark, my fierce ally.
It laughed as I fumbled, what a sight,
A little rascal igniting delight!

With colors bright, and patterns bold,
It held secrets, a story yet untold.
"Dance with me!" it teased and curled,
Bringing joy to this mundane world.

Just a trinket on a coat,
Yet it knew the fun to gloat.
A wink, a nod, from it to me,
Who knew style could be so carefree?

Magic Framed in Metal

A dot of spark on my lapel,
It giggles, casting quite a spell.
Each glance it casts steals the scene,
An impish grin, a playful sheen.

With every jingle in the sun,
It whispers, "Life's a game, let's run!"
It's shiny surface plays it cool,
But oh, the mischief in this jewel!

Adventurous flair, it leads the way,
Turning heads like a cabaret.
"Make a wish!" it dares with glee,
And I follow, wild and free!

In a world where dullness hovers,
It charms like laughter, oh how it discovers!
A flash of joy, bright as a spark,
It lights the path, igniting the dark.

Whispers of Adornment

On a coat, it found its home,
A cheeky little gem, no need to roam.
It chuckled softly, oh so sly,
As I strutted past, my head held high.

"Fancy me?" it toyed and glared,
With a wink, it said, "I'm perfectly paired!"
Its polished charm, a playful jest,
Turning the mundane into the best!

When boredom loomed in dreary haze,
It beamed and led in funny ways.
"Let's dance!" it hummed, and I complied,
With twirls and laughs, side by side.

In every gaze, it spun a tale,
Of laughter shared, and wearing the veil.
Though small, it knew the art of fun,
A laugh, a wink, a job well done!

Lament of the Forgotten Jewel

Once it glittered, full of cheer,
Now it sighs, "Where is the dear?"
Lonely on a dusty shelf,
A moan of charm, lost from itself.

It recalls the parties, oh those days,
Dancing with laughter in shimmering rays.
But now it ponders, 'Where's the fuss?'
In a world that forgot to discuss.

A once-proud gem, with stories galore,
It wonders if it matters anymore.
"Dust me off!" it cries in jest,
"Let's show them all how I am the best!"

But in silence, it waits in glee,
Hoping for moments, wild and free.
A memory trapped in fabric and thread,
Still dreaming of joy, though it's been misled.

Reflections of a Hidden Heart

A shiny gem on a coat's lapel,
Winks at me with a secret to tell.
Fashioned with flair, it's purely a jest,
Mocking my style, it doth love best.

In the mirror, it starts a dance,
Twinkling bright, it takes a chance.
'Look at you, in your plaid and stripe,'
The little sparkler teases with hype.

With every tilt in the morning light,
It chuckles softly, what a sight!
'Is that your look or a casual fright?'
Oh, the joy of its playful bite.

A mystery wrapped in shiny thread,
It whispers jokes that bounce in my head.
Fashion advice from a pin so small,
Who knew style tips could bring such a sprawl?

Luminous Secrets in Stillness

Nestled tight on a fancy dress,
Stealing attention with effortless finesse.
'What's your name, oh glittering star?'
Whispering tales from near and far.

It shimmies and shakes when I sit,
Playing tricks that perfectly fit.
'So misplaced among pearls and gold,'
'Just wait till the stories unfold.'

In quiet moments, it laughs with glee,
Polished smiles, oh so carefree!
'Did you think I'd let you go bare?'
This little jewel always has flair.

With its glow in the corner, it beckons me,
'Silly, don't doubt what you can see!'
A tiny comedic act right at hand,
Who knew accessories could be so grand?

The Glimmer of Untold Stories

Atop my lapel, it grins so wide,
Ready for giggles, with nothing to hide.
'Each flaw you see was a fashion hit,'
'Let's not pretend, we both know it's lit!'

In the spotlight, it shines quite bright,
Filling the room with pure delight.
'Can you dance? I think I can too!'
With a wink to the crowd, it joins in the crew.

Tales of mischief from ages ago,
Each shimmer and sparkle surely to show.
'Oh, darling, remember that day at the fair?'
Stories fly out like beads in the air.

From laughter's delight to whispers so sweet,
This tiny gem keeps my heart upbeat.
With a glimmer of stories its laughter provides,
It becomes my partner, my playful guide.

A Snapshot in Sparkle

Caught in a moment, a flash and a grin,
The little pin makes confusion begin.
'Did you steal the show or just your lunch?'
Innocent sparkle packs quite the punch.

With my outfit, it plays hide and seek,
Peeking out when I'm at my peak.
'Wearing me, you're dressed to impress!'
Oh, darling, it loves this silly mess.

Under the sun, it flickers and flips,
Sassy remarks with no boring quips.
'You think you dazzle? Well, take a look!'
Each twinkle tells more than pages in a book.

Snap! A picture, it strikes a pose,
Drawing attention wherever it goes.
A snapshot of joy that's fun from the heart,
This playful bauble is pure art!

Reflections in a Shining Heart

A sparkle caught my eye today,
A glimmer from a stash of clay.
I blinked and laughed at what I found,
A brooch that danced upon the ground.

It winked at me with a cheeky grin,
As if it knew the trouble I'm in.
I tried to wear it with some flair,
But ended up with a tangle in my hair.

Nestled among the socks and ties,
It murmured secrets, oh so sly.
"Wear me here, or wear me there,"
It sang, while twinkling with such flair.

A heart that shines but plays it smart,
It knows just how to steal the heart.
With every glance, my laughter swells,
As it spins tales that no one tells.

Secrets of the Stolen Gem

A sparkly thief with a flashy plan,
Darted away in the pocket of Stan.
It whispered secrets of treasures unplanned,
While tickling doubts with a ghostly hand.

In tea cups and crannies, the gem would hide,
Chasing the cat while I laughed till I cried.
"Oh, where did you go?" I asked with delight,
As it twinkled back from the darkest of night.

With tales of fortune and mischief galore,
It promised to sneak in and out through the door.
Who knew that a stone could be so uncouth,
Making me ponder the balance of truth?

It jibber-jabbered with glittery glee,
"I'm off to find more treasures — come, join me!"
And while it conspired to lead me astray,
I chuckled aloud at its silly display.

The Brocade of Memories

A fabric stitched with laughter's thread,
This trinket's tale is often misread.
Each twirl and twist of its shiny face,
Brings forth a memory of clumsy grace.

It once adorned a hat, bizarre and loud,
Of a party filled with a dancing crowd.
I tipped my head and it took a dive,
A poof of feathers! Oh, we felt alive!

In drawers of nostalgia, it loves to rest,
Among the mishaps, it feels so blessed.
With stories woven in colors bright,
It laughs at shadows that creep in the night.

Each embellishment tells of days gone by,
Of pie fights and pranks that made us fly.
So here's to the laughs, both silly and shy,
Captured in laughter — oh my! Oh my!

Enchantment in Enamel

A swirl of color with a cheeky wink,
It caught my heart before I could blink.
Embraced by laughter, it held a charm,
Dodging my clumsiness, safe from harm.

With polka dots and shiny flair,
It jiggles and jangles, dancing in air.
"Oh please, oh be careful!" the neighbors would yell,
As it flitted about casting a spell!

At picnics and outings, a star of the show,
To friends it promised, "Just watch me glow!"
With every adventure, it lived so free,
Claiming our days with wild jubilee.

And when I look back on the times we had,
This enamel enchantress makes me so glad.
With every giggle and every surprise,
It's a treasure of joy that never denies.

Glinting Secrets Beneath Fabric

Hidden gems in fabric's fold,
Whisper tales, both shy and bold.
Sparkling winks from threads at play,
Fashion's jest, in bright array.

Laughter dances, colors spin,
Each couture stitch a playful grin.
Worn by queens or just for fun,
These small delights, second to none.

Hooked on laughter, pinned in cheer,
Glimmering tales we love to wear.
Beneath the seams, a world of jest,
Charmed pinpoints radiate the best.

In the ballroom or café scene,
Each sparkling promise reigns serene.
For in each sparkle, joy resides,
Secret smiles the fabric hides.

A Whispered Elegance

Graceful whispers in a seam,
Elegant sparkle, a delightful dream.
Subtle nods from jewels bright,
Making fashion feel just right.

Every twirl, a giggle shared,
Threads entwined, no soul spared.
Chic and cheeky, oh what fun,
This playful fashion has just begun.

Dresses shimmer, shoes take flight,
A pin to prompt, what a sight!
Charmed by flair, we catch the tease,
In twinkling jewels, laughter frees.

Oh, how they sparkle, wink, and sway,
Each hidden gem has much to say.
With every grin, we join the dance,
A whispered elegance, a cheeky chance.

The Jewel's Silent Watch

A glimmer watches from afar,
Peeking out like a shooting star.
In the corner of one's eye,
It chuckles as we pass it by.

Patience worn, yet full of flair,
It's got the finest nature rare.
Wrapped in laughter, quiet pride,
In every moment, it's a guide.

With cheeky charm, it holds its seat,
Observing fashion's fun-filled beat.
Like a silent friend, it knows,
All the secrets that fabric sows.

Through the dance, through the spin,
The hidden views are lost within.
Yet ever-watchful, it will stay,
The jewel rolls smiles into the fray.

Adorned with Memories

Each trinket pinned tells a tale,
Of joyful moments that never pale.
Little chips of laughter's glow,
Worn like treasures, they steal the show.

Past gatherings where friends conspire,
Evenings lit by laughter's fire.
A playful nudge from a shining piece,
In every glance, sweet memories cease.

Faded fabric, yet bright the hue,
Embroidered with stories, both old and new.
Fashion's laughter wrapped so tight,
Adorned with memories, pure delight.

In every brooch, a hero's quest,
Championing laughter, never rest.
For beauty's held in playful threads,
In every moment, joy spreads.

The Charm of Hidden Narratives

On the shelf, it sparkles bright,
A story wrapped in whimsy light.
It whispers tales of grand old schemes,
Of dapper cats and midnight dreams.

A hidden pin with secrets tight,
Dances with laughter in the night.
It snickers softly, what a tease,
A brooch with more than just a breeze.

Each glance a giggle, every turn,
A riddle waits, a twist to learn.
It winks and nudges, a quiet jest,
"It's just a pin, but I'm the best!"

A collage of quirks in a silver frame,
Life's little jesters play their game.
With every clasp, a tale unfolds,
Of funny quirks and memories bold.

Brocade Dreams and Distant Memories

In satin dreams, where laughter breathes,
A charm bestowed that loves to tease.
Patterns shift in joyous play,
As brocade spins its tales away.

Each stitch a wink, each thread a jest,
Memories dance in fabric's chest.
Echoes of laughter, whispers of cheer,
Adventures saved, tucked away near.

A tapestry of comical sights,
Adorning vestiges of quiet nights.
With every glance, a chuckle shared,
For those who've danced and dared, and dared.

In the folds, the stories dwell,
Of brocade treasures that time shall tell.
Funny enough to make you sigh,
Remembered moments that never die.

Gaze of Metallic Shadows

A shimmer caught in playful light,
Shadows giggle, but out of sight.
In every twinkle, mischief sways,
As metallic spirits weave their plays.

A glance reveals a cheeky smile,
In the reflections, they lie awhile.
Glimmers tease with witty charms,
Wrapped around in playful arms.

Each fold a smile, each shine a laugh,
Echoing whispers of an old photograph.
It nudges you with each little rise,
A mischievous wink, a quick surprise.

So here it lies, with tales to impart,
A treasure hidden, a gleaming heart.
Steel and silver in silly play,
In shadows dancing, they find their way.

An Echo in the Fabric

With stitches fine, a joke is spun,
In fibers soft, where tales are fun.
An echo muffled, shy and shy,
Of charms and giggles wrapped nearby.

It twirls in circles, laughing bright,
With seams that shimmer and catch the light.
Each twine a whisper, each knot a grin,
A lining where odd anecdotes begin.

Hidden gems in fabric's hold,
Mysteries wrapped in the threads of old.
The echo starts, a silly tease,
"Just look at me, I'm sure to please!"

So take a moment, pause and gaze,
At all the fun in woven rays.
For laughter lies in every seam,
A patchwork quilt of a joyful dream.

A Light Beyond Our Time

In a drawer, a sparkly friend,
Whispers of laughter, twists that bend.
It winks at socks, it rolls its eyes,
A pin that claims the biggest lies.

On a hat, it's quite the show,
Says, "Who needs fashion? Let's just glow!"
With rhinestones bright and colors bold,
It tells tall tales from days of old.

Adorning scarves, it steals the scene,
"I'm splendid!" it shrieks, like a queen.
But one wrong hook, and off it flies,
Chasing a cat—oh, what a surprise!

When friends drop by and take a glance,
They burst in giggles, start to dance.
A cherished relic, or just a prank?
It's those brooches, we should thank!

Enigmatic Luster

In the attic, dust does stray,
A curious find from yesterday.
A shiny thing with stories ripe,
It winks and grins, plays the type.

It sparkles bright like morning dew,
Suggesting secrets; what's it due?
Is it a treasure, or just a joke?
This whimsically shimmering cloak!

At garden parties, it finds its place,
Among the tea cups, with poise and grace.
While doing a dance, it pops and gleams,
Transforming talks into wild dreams!

And when the moonlight paints the night,
It giggles soft, a charming sight.
This whimsical jewel will surely astound,
With tales of mischief unbound!

The Spirit of Past Fancies

A trinket lost, yet never gone,
Time-traveling with its golden dawn.
Tickling hearts with tales of flair,
This playful gem loves to declare.

It jests with hats and given fright,
To stiff old suits—oh what a sight!
Unfurls those laps, creates a stir,
Like a clown in polka dots, it's a blur!

Worn by grandmas, worn by pets,
Invisible strings and silly bets.
With every twinkle, chuckles rise,
Who knew fashion could wear such disguise?

Inside the closet, chaos reigns,
A dance of colors, mischief gains.
And just like that, with glee, it prances,
We're left enchanted by wild glances!

Ciphers in Brightness

A curious pin beneath the bed,
Holds secrets of the foolishly wed.
With ribbons frayed and colors tossed,
It laughs at the cost of looks long lost.

A conversation with mismatched socks,
How it teases clocks that just can't talk.
Spills confetti on formal wear,
Was it meant for glam, or a joke laid bare?

With every tilt, a wink is shared,
A fashion faux pas? Not that it cared.
It turns the mundane to merry sights,
Wielding humor on glittering nights!

In shadows deep, it knows the jest,
A cheerful spirit, never stressed.
So here's to a brooch with charms so spry,
With laughter wrapped in a sparkling tie!

Tales Adorning the Heart

A shiny trinket on my coat,
It winks at folks, it seems to gloat.
"Look at me, I'm such a star!"
While inwardly I'm a bit bizarre.

At parties, it steals every show,
With stories only I can know.
A chatty clasp, it squeaks and beams,
Creating laughter from my dreams.

When I trip and tumble down,
It giggles loud, it wears a crown.
"I've seen better, come take a peek,"
Sassy kin, such a cheeky freak.

Yet in the day, when all is calm,
My gem's a friend, my heart it charms.
Through laughter, joy, and silly dare,
This tale adorns my coat with flair.

Gaze of the Authentic

A quirky pin upon my chest,
It nods and winks, it's truly best.
"I know your secrets, oh dear friend,"
It chuckles gently at each bend.

Beneath the light, it has a glow,
It's judging outfits, just so you know.
"Is that what you wore to the big dance?"
With playful laughter, it takes its stance.

I swear it rolls its tiny eyes,
At every fashion faux pas that lies.
"Darling, darling, is that your choice?"
In my reflection, I hear its voice.

Yet as the night begins to fade,
We laugh together at love's charade.
For through my wardrobe's endless chase,
Shines the truth of style in its embrace.

The Silence of Adorned Memories

Resting lightly, it's quiet tonight,
This wink of shimmer, oh what a sight!
It knows my tales, my laughs, my tears,
A silent witness through all the years.

In moments bright and in times so low,
It gleams with secrets only we know.
"Remember when you danced so bold?"
It whispers softly, stories retold.

While folks just see a bit of flair,
It keeps the giggles, the pout, the scare.
"You tripped on air, and I laughed too,"
Such silly times, it's been our glue.

Yet as I wear it day by day,
It sparkles gently, come what may.
Each glance a nudge, a chuckle shared,
In quiet joy, our past is bared.

A Gem's Timeless Vigil

On my lapel, a gem does sit,
With glossy gleam, it's quite a hit.
"I'm watching you, don't mess it up,"
It teases me, this little cup.

In crowded rooms, it knows my style,
Winking softly, it plays the while.
"That shirt again? Oh dear, oh me!"
Its humor dances, wild and free.

When I'm caught in awkward glares,
It helps me smile and loses cares.
"Life's too short, just strike a pose!"
It shouts for joy, as laughter flows.

Through every trend and fashion twist,
It keeps our spirits in a tryst.
With every glance, it gives a cheer,
A magic gem, forever near.

Artistry in Stillness

A shiny gem on fabric holds,
Winking secrets, stories told.
It giggles with each passing glance,
What a charming little dance!

A sparkle here, a twinkle there,
Making folks stop, pause, and stare.
"What's that glimmer?" they inquire,
Just a brooch with witty fire!

It sits so proud, a sassy queen,
Laughing at the in-between.
Adorning jackets, hats, and ties,
With a smirk that amplifies!

Oh, the life it could have led,
If only words spilled from its thread.
Instead, it winks and keeps it sly,
A jewel that knows how to apply!

Stories in Bright Colors

Once a brooch in shades so bold,
Fancied tales of knights of old.
With reds and greens and blues that shine,
Each hue could twist a clever line!

It sparkles bright in morning sun,
Whispering jokes, just for fun.
"I'm not just metal, set me free!"
It'd shout, while folks just sip their tea.

Oh, the snapshots that it holds,
Of quirky parties, dances, and folds.
Beneath the wear, a heart so spry,
Sharing laughter as time goes by!

A button here, a pin so sweet,
Fancy accessories can't compete.
For in its shimmer lies a tale,
A funny life that will prevail!

Guardian of Dreams

A guardian with a shiny shield,
Hiding jokes that are concealed.
It wears a smile, so sly and bright,
Guarding dreams through the night!

It twists and turns in moonlit glow,
Winking at secrets only it knows.
With a quirky charm, it likes to tease,
A tiny jester with perfect ease!

"I guard your hopes, just watch and see,"
It promises with glee and giddy.
When morning breaks, it chuckles loud,
For all the dreams it has allowed.

So, here it sits, so brave and bold,
In shadows of glitter, stories told.
An escort through your sleep, it beams,
Oh, the funny world of dreams!

Threads of Nostalgia

A vintage pin, so full of cheer,
Hugs the fabric, ever near.
With age comes wisdom, so they say,
In threads of laughter, come what may!

Through every stitch and every seam,
It carries echoes of a dream.
A time when puns were all the rage,
And belly laughs graced every stage!

It sparkles with a wink so sly,
Remembering moments passing by.
Each wearer's tale a funny twist,
A bond of joy that can't be missed!

So cherish now this little sprite,
A thread of memories, pure delight.
In nostalgia's gaze, it brings a grin,
For every laugh where joy begins!

Veiled Sparkle

A shiny gem upon my dress,
It winks at folks, I must confess.
"Don't touch me there!" it seems to say,
While I just laugh and walk away.

A tiny creature, oh so proud,
It's got a grin that's far too loud.
This little thing, a charming tease,
Mocks the socks I wear with ease.

When friends come round, it steals the show,
I roll my eyes, but still I glow.
How can a thing so small and neat,
Bring all my fashion sense to defeat?

Yet here we are, a perfect pair,
In silly games, it leads the flair.
With sparkle bright, it takes the lead,
In wardrobe wars, I take the heed!

Legends Hidden in Adornment

Once a tale of princess and knight,
Was told by my pin in the soft moonlight.
It sighed and whispered with such great flair,
Of jewels and banquets, beyond compare.

It tangle-danced in vintage gold,
Of secret stories, fun and bold.
With tiny laughter, it claims its throne,
This brooch is more than just a stone.

I swear that it can cast a spell,
With every glance, folks seem to dwell.
As they investigate with furrowed brow,
"Hmmm, what secrets does it allow?"

In silly tales, it plays the part,
A storytelling work of art.
As legends bloom from threads and seams,
My tiny pin just lives in dreams.

The Echo of Intricate Design

An echo of fun in metal's clasp,
With playful twists, it's hard to grasp.
One moment here, the next it flies,
With mischief wrapped within its guise.

It wiggles freely, begging to play,
On collar or coat, it steals the day.
In laughter's name, we spin and twirl,
This lively pin, a joy to swirl.

I'd like to think it's wise and keen,
In chuckles shared, it steals the scene.
"Oh, don't be shy, come take a look!"
It beams so bright, like a storybook.

In every twist, a quirk you'll find,
With every glance, a wink entwined.
Its voice, though silent, shouts with glee,
An echo of fun for you and me!

Shimmering Dreams of Yesteryear

In dreams of past that sparkle bright,
A brooch appears, a pure delight.
It nods and giggles at old attire,
With tales so wild, one can't retire.

It sparkles softly, like a tease,
Nibbling at memories, aiming to please.
The dance it leads, an old-time song,
Where everything quirky seems to belong.

A shimmer here, a twist of fate,
Each pinning leads to laughs and weight.
"Do you remember when you wore this?"
A wink, a wiggle, a perfect bliss.

So here I am, with past in tow,
This gleaming nugget puts on a show.
In shimmering dreams, I find my cheer,
As laughter echoes throughout the year!

A Spark in the Silken Veil

A shimmer caught in the morning light,
Twirling threads, an unexpected sight.
The cat leaps high, with a curious meow,
Draped in fabric, pretending to bow.

A twist of fate, a sunbeam's tease,
A button found where it shouldn't be.
The laughter rings as the dog joins in,
Chasing shadows with a goofy grin.

The seamstress sighs, her work undone,
With every stitch, a tale begun.
A spark of mischief, a fraying thread,
In silken layers, all secrets spread.

With every gaze, the folly grows,
A fashion faux pas, as everyone knows.
Yet even in chaos, joy prevails,
In every twinkle, a story sails.

Lost Gems, Found Dreams

A treasure hunt in the attic's gloom,
Old boxes whisper, making room.
A jigsaw piece, a missing jewel,
Who knew the cat could be such a fool?

The sparkle gleams from the dusty shelf,
An old necklace, but wait... it's a belt!
Tangled strands that once were fine,
Now a crown for the canine divine.

Under floorboards, a glimmering chase,
Marbles and ribbons, a childhood place.
The laughter echoes with each new find,
A broken bracelet, yet joy unconfined.

So let's gather the bits of our past,
With every misfit, fun is amassed.
A quirky treasure, a dream it seems,
In lost gems, we find silly dreams.

Silhouettes beneath the Surface

In puddles deep, reflections play,
Round and round in a comical way.
A duck on a quest, with quacks so bold,
Dancing with shadows, uncontrolled.

Umbrellas up, the rain takes flight,
As kids splash gleefully, oh what a sight!
Each silhouette, a story to claim,
In the whimsical world of the puddle game.

A top hat, a cane, what a fine disguise,
The dog's dapper dance, oh how he tries!
With every leap, a giggle erupts,
In the rain's embrace, laughter erupts.

So let's celebrate all forms of fun,
In every puddle, a race to run.
With silly shapes and splashes wide,
The joy we find, our world confides.

The Inanimate Witness

Upon the shelf, a porcelain cat,
Sitting quite still, thinking 'What's that?'
With a poky twig, the child does play,
While the cat judges in its own way.

A bowl of fruit, now a hat for the clown,
As laughter spills all over town.
Each item gleams with a quirky charm,
Unmoved by chaos, ensured no harm.

The teapot grins, quite full of glee,
While socks embark on a dance spree.
With a wink to the clock and a tap on the wall,
The day's delightful, enchanting all.

Though not alive, they are full of cheer,
In every nook, magic is near.
Behind every scene, the laughter thrives,
In inanimate tales, our joy survives.

The Radiant Watcher

Upon the lapel, a twinkle bright,
Glimmers and giggles, a curious sight.
It winks at the world with a cheeky grin,
Caught in the chaos, it dance within.

A rustle of fabric, it's lost in the fray,
Peeking at secrets, come what may.
It chuckles aloud with a mischievous flair,
Beware of the tales it might dare to share!

A dog with a bow tie, a cat in a hat,
This lively observer is loving that.
In a whirlwind of nonsense, it finds delight,
Oh, what a show on this silly night!

So lift up your chin, let your laughter unfold,
In the company of shiny stories told.
With a wink and a nod, it's ever so bold,
The radiant watcher, forever on hold.

Intricate Patterns of Remembrance

Twisted and tangled, a fashion faux pas,
With petals and polka dots, oh dear, how bizarre!
Memories flutter like moths in the light,
Each sparkle and shimmer, an unforgettable sight.

It shifts to the left, then suddenly right,
Combining odd colors with sheer delight.
"Oh look at me now!" it proclaims with a jest,
A fashion-forward rebel, it's truly the best!

Past moments they whisper, a series of pranks,
A riddle of fabric, fluffed up with thanks.
Each curve tells a story that's hard to track,
If only they could, they'd send tales back!

So gather around, let nostalgia flow,
In patterns of laughter, its colors will glow.
With giggles and memories, together we sway,
Intricate tapestries from yesterday's play.

The Luster of Silent Stories

In pins and in jewels, stories reside,
Whispers of laughter no one can hide.
Glimmers of moments locked tight in its shell,
A quiet spectator, observing all well.

At parties it chuckles, tries not to shout,
While wearing a flower, it dances about.
With every twist and a playful little spin,
It keeps all the secrets tucked snugly within.

A clink and a clang whenever it moves,
Absorbing the mischief that life always proves.
It beams at the friendships, the quirks that we show,
The luster of memories that help us all grow.

So here's to the shine, the quiet delight,
Of stories amassed in the soft golden light.
In the world of the bold, it prefers to recline,
The subtle enchanter, simply divine.

Whispering Silhouettes

Dancing in shadows, they can never be still,
Echoes of laughter, drifting at will.
Silhouettes chatter in a breezy embrace,
Each sparkle a secret, a shimmering grace.

With a tip and a turn, they wobble and sway,
In a world of colorful chaos at play.
"Oh what a night!" they giggle and cheer,
Riding on whimsy, no worry or fear!

While onlookers ponder, quite puzzled and lost,
What tales could emerge at such humorous cost?
A playful alignment, a misfit parade,
Whispering silhouettes, bright memories made.

So let's raise a laugh to our sparkling friends,
In moments of joy, their magic transcends.
With whispers that tickle, they charm without fail,
In a world of pure whimsy, let's set sail!

Chronology of a Gleaming Memory

In a drawer, a trinket hides,
Sparkles wink, where humor resides.
Each pin and clasp tells a tale,
Of fashion flops, and that one whale.

Glimmers catch the light's sweet tease,
Old Aunt Gertie's sneezes were a breeze.
A dance of quirks on every pin,
Laughter echoes; let the fun begin.

A shiny star, a comet bright,
Winks at you with pure delight.
Oh, the stories they could share,
As they poke fun, with style and flair.

Yet who would think, in all that bling,
A circus act that starts to sing?
The metallic laughter fills the room,
As history parades—a peekaboo bloom.

The Unseen Eyes of History

In shadows cast by jewel's glow,
A laughing crowd begins to flow.
Old relics spark in a cheeky way,
They giggle softly, come what may.

Each glint a wink from days of yore,
Hats off to the styles that we abhor.
A brooch so fierce, yet rather shy,
Rolls its eyes as fashions fly by.

Poking fun at every fad,
Fashion faux pas make them glad.
These sparkling jesters, quite the crew,
Sharing tales with every hue.

Oh, how they twinkle, tease, and play,
Unseen eyes watching the fray.
What's past is jest, in glimmer and glance,
In the history books, they've stolen the dance.

Elegies of the Ornate

In a box of treasures where memories dwell,
Lies beadwork that casts a spell.
Each little gem, a quirky cheer,
Recites tales of laughter, year by year.

A flourish here, a swirl there,
The elegance winks, beyond compare.
Ode to the lace, a memorial of grace,
Yet all it recalls is a twist on a face.

Frayed edges speak of an age gone by,
Where balloons popped as jokes took flight.
Jest upon jest, the satin gleams,
In the heart of whimsy, laughter beams.

The past may whisper, but make no mistake,
These treasures fancy, make no heartbreak.
In every pin, a giggle, a sway,
Ornate elegies of jests on display.

The Hidden Voices of Sparkle

Beneath the glam of shiny bits,
Lies dialogue wrapped in witty skits.
Each shimmer dances in playful voice,
Telling tales that make you rejoice.

A glittery crowd of charming souls,
Whispers of laughter, eccentric roles.
With every clasp, a secret wink,
Encouraging you all to think.

A sapphire glare, a ruby smirk,
Fashion's jesters, oh how they lurk.
They recommend chaos with stylish flair,
In the world of shimmer, beware, beware!

So let them sparkle, those playful gems,
In the orchestra of laughter, each one condemns.
Suit up in joy, never in fright,
For hidden voices bring pure delight.

A Glimmer Through Time

A jewel perched high, what a sight,
Winking from shadows, with delight.
Whispers of laughter, it spreads around,
With secrets of ages, forever unbound.

Each sparkle a giggle, each twist a jest,
A playful spirit, never at rest.
Hiding in pockets, it plans a good prank,
Making us wonder, then laughing, we thank.

Oh, how it twinkles in bright sunny rays,
Fooling the sun to dance in its blaze.
The fabric of time, it patches with cheer,
A glimmer of mischief that's always near.

So here's to the bauble, a rogue in disguise,
Taking us back with its humorous lies.
In the story of fashion, it plays a grand role,
A glimmering treasure, a jester's sole goal.

Capturing the Lost Light

In a drawer sat treasures, buried in dust,
With giggles and glints, it felt like a must.
The charm with a sass, it prances around,
Like a puppy that's found its long-lost sound.

Tickles of laughter, it tugs at our hearts,
Ensnaring our joy, with flamboyant arts.
Who knew a clasp could cause such a ruckus?
With each shining flash, it always will trust us.

Capturing sunlight, in playful disguise,
It winks at our woes and lifts up our sighs.
"Wear me," it giggles, "we'll have quite a blast,
You'll forget all your troubles, forget all the past!"

So let us adorn it, with flair and with pride,
And dance with this trinket, our laughter our guide.
Whirling through moments, caught under its light,
In this whimsical venture, everything feels right.

Odes to Ornamentation

Oh, dapper distraction, you shine and you beam,
A curious critter in fashion's grand theme.
With curls and with swirls, you prance on my chest,
Bringing forth chuckles, oh, you're quite the jest!

A heart or a star, it matters not here,
You tickle our fancies, you draw us near.
In chaos you flourish, a master at play,
Making us giggle on any old day.

Draped over velvet, or clinging to lace,
You play peek-a-boo in this stylish rat race.
Your sass has a license, to twirl and to spin,
A dance of adornment where laughter will win.

So cheers to you, sparkles, in this ode sung,
For bringing us joy, like brightly spun tongue.
You paint our existence with whimsical glee,
Forever we treasure this jubilant spree.

The Brooch's Silent Watch

Upon the lapel, a silent delight,
Winking at passerby, causing a fright.
With no word to utter, it holds back its tease,
But giggles emerge with a rustle of breeze.

A prisoner of whimsy, it captures the jest,
Always observing, a true little pest.
From parties to picnics, it keeps its own score,
Rolling its eyes as it watches us snore.

Fashion's best keeper of secrets and fun,
It knows all the stories, beneath the hot sun.
With each tilt and shimmer, it sparks up a chat,
Bringing forth laughter, with a wink and a spat.

So here's to the treasure that sits and it spies,
A notorious jewel with mischievous eyes.
It whispers in colors, it chuckles in gold,
Forever enchanting, forever retold.

A Glimpse Beyond the Surface

A shiny pin with tales to tell,
It sparkles bright, but gritty as well.
Once it danced in a fancy ball,
Now it's stuck to the fridge in the hall.

Brooch of laughter and whimsy's lore,
Whispers secrets of days before.
It sings of adventures, wild and free,
A map of memories, just wait and see!

One day worn by a stylish dame,
The next, it hangs in a dusty frame.
Oh, the places it wanted to roam,
Now it's a fixture, far from its home.

But fear not, dear pin, your worth isn't gone,
In the world of laughter, you still shine on!
So raise a toast for your glimmering art,
For beauty and fun live in every part.

Luminous Tales Untold

Once a focal piece of jubilation,
Now a relic in need of salvation.
Glittering stories on fabric spun,
Holding moments of laughter and fun.

A daisy here, a heart shaped there,
This gem had flair, but now it's rare.
With its crooked pin and a winking eye,
It giggles softly, oh my, oh my!

It wanted to sparkle, to dazzle the crowd,
Now it just dreams, all alone and proud.
But memories shine brighter than gold,
In the oddest of places, laughter unfolds.

Don't overlook what's lost in the past,
For humor and joy are meant to last.
So laugh with the jewels, both old and new,
Life's a funny dance, just enjoy the view!

Jewelry of the Unforgotten

In corners dusty, it waits with glee,
Worn by a cat on a wild spree.
Once sophisticated, now a bit bent,
It chuckles soft, 'What a life I've spent!'

Each tangle and twist a story unique,
Of dances and whims, with a humorous streak.
An heirloom of giggles, each facet a jest,
No wonder it rests, it's earned its quest!

Brooch of the moment, unique as can be,
Sharing a tale, oh the irony!
Clipped on pajamas, at home with a grin,
Fashion statements may come, but this soul wears thin.

Let's cherish the jewels in our everyday,
For laughter and memories are here to stay.
So dust off that treasure and give it a spin,
Make way for the chuckles, let the fun begin!

The Heart of Immaculate Design

A cluster of gems with a wink in the light,
Once a fashionista's glittering delight.
Now it rests quietly, oh what a shame,
Waiting for parties to play the old game.

Once it twinkled in high society style,
Now is a guardian of laughter's guile.
A tacky old pin, but never too late,
To find its charm in a whimsical fate.

Resting on collars or hats with a flair,
Creating a ruckus, spreading its cheer.
Let's wear it with laughter, not mind how it looks,
For the heart of its story fills up all the books!

So here's to old friends, both shiny and bold,
With laughter and stories, a bond to uphold.
Dress up your day with a sprinkle of cheer,
For life is a brooch, so let's hold it dear!

Locket of Longing

In a locket, secrets swirl,
A tiny picture of a girl.
She's all smiles, yet I can't see,
Why she chose to hide from me.

Each clasp a giggle, each hinge a sigh,
What's in there? Oh my, oh my!
A heart, a wish, or just a hair?
Oh, the mysteries that we share!

It jingles loud when I take a stroll,
Drawing stares like I'm on a roll.
Does it think it's quite the show?
Well, I can't take it off, you know!

With a wink and a sparkle bright,
It whispers tales both day and night.
In this little chest of dreams,
Love's in the air, or so it seems!

Beneath the Surface of Sparkle

Beneath the shine, what do I find?
A million secrets intertwined.
A sparkle here, a wink from there,
    Is it magic or just flair?

They twinkle, dance, and catch the eye,
Oh, such laughter, let's not be shy!
A diamond winks, a ruby grins,
What's hidden there? Let the giggles begin!

They gossip loud, in whispers sweet,
The stories shared are quite the treat.
Around the necks, they prance and play,
Who knew jewels could be this way?

Underneath the glimmering haze,
Lies a world of funny ways.
With each glitter, jesting winds,
Together, let's see what this spins!

Beauty Caught in Time

Caught in a frame of vintage grace,
A snapshot, oh what a funny face!
Eyelashes exaggerated, smiles so wide,
What were we thinking? Oh, the pride!

Tick-tock goes the clock, it hums a tune,
"Oh, look at me!" sings the old cartoon.
Time moves fast, but what a ride,
Memories play a silly side.

Each tick again retells that jest,
In every glance, we find our best.
Caught in time, those silly days,
Oh how we loved to laugh and play!

With every wrinkle, laughter's mark,
The beautiful storms leave a little spark.
Forever framed, those funny scenes,
In our hearts, we hold our dreams!

The Jewel's Silent Witness

In silence sits a gem so bright,
Watching us dance through day and night.
A twinkle here, a nod of cheer,
What tales it holds, we want to hear!

Amid the laughter, it gives a wink,
While we are lost in thoughts to think.
"Oh, remember that?" it seems to say,
As we tumble through the silly fray.

Its colors flash like jokes we tell,
Mixed with memories, all is swell!
A quiet laugh in every shine,
Oh, the fun that's truly divine!

So let it sparkle, let it gleam,
In its presence, we all beam.
A jewel so wise, yet full of cheer,
Our silent witness, always near!

Intricacies of a Hidden Story

In a garden of pins and chains,
Each twist, a tale that remains.
A rogue clasp, with winks and grins,
Hides laughter beneath its skin.

Adventures in metal, who knew?
Tiny paths those curls pursue.
Whispers of fashion through the years,
Unveiling giggles mixed with tears.

A butterfly perched, ready to flee,
Wings of humor, wild and free.
With every sparkle, secrets tease,
While we laugh and wonder, "What's the key?"

Behind every backing, a jest or two,
With stitches and stories, all feel brand new.
They twinkle and dance, these gleeful things,
In the grand bazaar, where laughter sings.

Radiant Reflections of Longing

In a pinched pocket, a glimmer resides,
It wiggles and giggles, refusing to hide.
Adorned with memories, so bright and bold,
Yearning for laughter while stories unfold.

A glitzy charm with its shiny glare,
Mimics our dreams with whimsical flair.
It skips through moments, gleefully precise,
Winking at wishes, oh how nice, oh how nice!

Duplicity wraps with sparkles and spark,
This shiny companion, a quirky lark.
It's poking fun at our fancy regales,
As it giggles in rhythm, and silently wails.

Each twinkle a nod, each shimmer a sigh,
Echoes of laughter that never say why.
In the glow of the night, with a wink and a shout,
Longing for joy that we live without doubt.

The Keepers of Forgotten Tales

Nestled in velvet, a pin's little dream,
With tales to tell, and laughter to beam.
Once lost in a cupboard, now found in a spree,
With yarns spun from laughter, oh, let it be!

Round and round, it twists and plays,
The past is alive in its shimmering ways.
It chuckles at fashion, and hats of old,
Keeps secrets of lives, both timid and bold.

Beneath the surface, the stories collide,
With humor, they tumble like jewels in stride.
Each gleaming pawn a character fine,
In the game of old, it's all about time.

They giggle at wrinkles and side-eyes of chance,
The keepers of secrets, in their fancy dance.
With every clasp, their stories relay,
And we can't help but learn to play.

Secrets Wrapped in Luster

Beneath the shimmer, a jest takes hold,
Wrapped in a luster, both funny and bold.
A whimsical wink from a heart of gold,
In the laugh of the clasp, secrets unfold.

With charms that dangle, and jests that soar,
Every sparkle a grin, an open door.
In the glinting light, dig deeper still,
Beneath every surface, more laughter to spill.

A hidden layer, a puzzle to piece,
There's humor in stories that never cease.
They play tag with memory, hide-and-seek fun,
Wrapped tight in elegance, for everyone.

So we gather 'round, these treasures of glee,
With echoes of laughter, forever to be.
With every glance, we unwrap a joke,
In the colorful world where secrets provoke.

Gemstone Eyes and Timeless Truths

A gem in a shop, oh what a sight,
Winking at me with joy and delight.
It knows all my secrets, or so it seems,
Whispers of nonsense, mixed with my dreams.

I wear it with pride, although it just sits,
A companion in awkward, a friend made of bits.
With laughs and with quirks, together we shine,
In the grand game of life, you're my grand design.

Its sparkle proposes, 'Come dance through the night,'
While I'm stuck in pajamas, what a daft plight!
Yet still I imagine, with charm and with grace,
That we're the bold figures in a wild dream race.

So here's to the trinkets, to stories unfold,
To gemstones that watch, and the laughter they hold.
In this zany adventure, come join in the cheer,
For life is a jewel, and I hold it near.

The Quiet Oracle of Silver and Stone

In corners it sits, wise and serene,
Collecting my thoughts, like a silent machine.
With flickers of madness, it sparkles with truth,
Implores me to share all my tales of youth.

It nods at my fashion, a bit of a tease,
Promising wisdom like running through cheese.
The laughter we share, in whispers so bold,
Like secrets unspoke, wrapped in shimmering gold.

Once it predicted I'd wear polka dots,
A fashion disaster, oh what were the odds?
Yet here I am, posing in stripes with a grin,
Embracing the chaos that lies deep within.

So let it be known, in this shiny retreat,
That even a stone can dance to the beat.
With laughter as fuel, and style as our guise,
Together we'll shine, oh, what a surprise!

Threads of Glamour and Remembrance

Stitched with some humor, each thread's a laugh,
Tales woven with hiccups, oh what a gaff.
With glamour we twirl, like leaves in the breeze,
Each stitch is a memory, each giggle's a tease.

Oh draped in the fabric of whimsical skies,
I prance through the world, to peeks and to sighs.
With glamour in mind, and stitches so tight,
We're fashioning joy, with colors so bright.

So here's to the weavings that play with our hearts,
A patchwork of laughter, where silliness starts.
Each thread tells a story, each knot brings a grin,
In the quilt of existence, let the fun begin!

Stitched up with care, we dance in delight,
Through fabric and laughter, we'll twirl into night.
As threads intertwine, in a glorious mess,
We'll wear our mishaps like crowns, and impress!

Unearthed Elegance

From depths of the earth, peek-a-boo gems,
Whispering elegance, like cheeky little hems.
They play hide and seek with the light and the dirt,
Dripping with laughter, beneath layers of hurt.

With sparkle and sass, they're ready to tease,
Each one a character that aims to please.
In this ball of confusion, they shine oh so bright,
Turning everyday chaos into pure delight.

They flaunt their allure, with a twinkle and pun,
As if to declare that the party's begun.
Unearthed, unexpected, they drive us to cackle,
Who knew elegance lived in such a fine shackled?

So here's to the gems, the quirky and bold,
Mischievous treasures, their secrets unfold.
With laughter as currency, dancing we'll go,
In this wild embrace, let the elegance flow!

Gems of Silent Desires

In the drawer, the sparkles hide,
Whispers of dreams that never died.
A little gem with a cheeky grin,
Laughing softly at where it's been.

A sassy ruby, a playful tease,
Caught in a dance with the lightest breeze.
It winks at us from the velvet deep,
Saying secrets, daring us to peep.

Emerald eyes twinkle so bright,
Planning mischief beneath the night.
They giggle at tales of glitzy glows,
And all the places where no one goes.

Though they rest in a shadowy cave,
In every twinkle, there's laughter to save.
For in their silence, there's joy to find,
Gems of hopes and dreams entwined.

LooK! A Memory in Gold

A locket that holds a secret smile,
Swings from a chain, in a quirky style.
With each clang, it winks at the day,
Reminding us of laughs on display.

Beneath the dust, a gleam does stir,
Telling tales of an old great fur.
It chuckles about the days gone by,
When clumsy hands made it fly high.

A sprinkle of shine, it plays its part,
With glittering tales that tickle the heart.
In a world of shiny, it steals the show,
A memory wrapped in a bright gold glow.

As friends gather 'round with stories to swap,
This charm knows when it's time to hop.
And with a laugh, it shimmies so bold,
Celebrating moments, like tales of old.

The Charm of Abandoned Treasures

In a box of wonders, things may lie,
Each one awaits with a hopeful sigh.
A button, a bead, a piece of lace,
Little treasures, each with a face.

They speak in colors, they giggle with glee,
Chasing the cats that dance by the tree.
Lost ornaments from a festive night,
Now playfully plotting their next flight.

A shell from the beach with a wink and a nudge,
Recalls the waves, like a friendly judge.
Whispers of joy in a sunlit flare,
Summoning laughter to fill the air.

As dust settles, these charms cheerfully roam,
Making a laugh of their worn-out home.
Each one a beacon of mischievous cheer,
Abandoned, but never truly austere.

Musings of Iridescent Shadows

In corners dim, the shadows play,
With colors swirling in a funny way.
They tumble and twist, a merry band,
Frolicking in light, a joyful strand.

As they gossip in a silvery hue,
They tickle the air; oh, what a view!
A bounce of cobalt, a splash of lime,
Creating a ruckus, stealing the time.

Their laughter echoes off the walls,
With secrets wrapped in shimmery stalls.
They dance like sprites, each cheerfully bold,
In whimsical flights, their stories unfold.

A party of hues, where colors collide,
In shadows' embrace, they love to abide.
With each flicker, a chuckling song,
In iridescence, they all belong.

Secrets Safeguarded in Sparkles

In the jewelry box, a secret lies,
A sparkly friend with mischief in its eyes.
It winks at the socks, it giggles with pride,
A whimsical charm that can't be denied.

Tiny gems whisper giggles so bright,
As they plot to dance under the moonlight.
With every twist, they laugh and they twine,
Creating a ruckus, one sparkling line.

It tugs at the blouse with a cheeky grin,
Saying, "Let's get this party to begin!"
Each clasp and each pin, a playful encore,
A dazzling ensemble you simply can't ignore.

So here's to the joy that sparkles and plays,
In the world of accessories, let laughter blaze.
For in the glint of a sparkle's embrace,
Lies a treasure of joy, a mischievous grace.

A Tapestry of Glances and Glimmers

In a flutter of fabric, the glimmers convene,
Creating a drama, a whimsical scene.
They poke and they prod, in a fabric parade,
A riotous gathering where laughter won't fade.

With every glance tossed, like confetti in air,
They conjure up giggles, a spectacle rare.
The beads roll their eyes, while sequins take flight,
In a catwalk of chaos that sparkles so bright.

"Look over there!" sings a charm with delight,
"Did you see that sock? Isn't it a sight?"
They shimmy and shake, the jewels have their say,
As fashion and humor join in the ballet.

Together they spin, a shimmering tease,
Crafting a tapestry sure to appease.
So raise up your glass to the glimmers that play,
In this realm of laughter, forever we'll stay.

The Watcher's Whisper on Fabric

A watchful little gem lays low on the lace,
With secrets aplenty, it shares with grace.
"Oh dear," it chuckles, "look who's wearing me,
A mismatched outfit, how funny it be!"

Each thread holds a joke, a sparkling jest,
As the fabric behaves like it just passed a test.
The patterns swap stories, the colors unite,
In this whimsical world, everything's bright.

"Hey, over there," whispers a cheeky clasp,
"Did you catch the bow? It's giving a rasp!"
They giggle and titter, such joy on display,
In the mischief of fashion, let giggles sway.

So listen closely, oh wearers so bold,
To the tales that are spun in the fabrics of gold.
Wearing laughter's delight as our finest attire,
We'll dance with the gems, let the fun never tire.

Sparkling Memories in Disguise

In the corner of the room, a treasure awaits,
Gems hiding stories behind silver gates.
With laughter echoing, they wait for a spark,
Planning a party when it gets dark.

The pearl sparkles soft, whispers, "Come near!
I've got jest-filled tales you'll want to hear."
The diamonds all twinkle, with mischievous flair,
While the rubies blush red for the fun in the air.

"Let's dress up the couch, let's dazzle the tea!
Fashionable flair is the way it should be!"
Each sparkle a memory, each shine a delight,
They waltz on the fabric, in laughter's pure light.

So join in the merriment, don't shy away,
For the sparkle of joy is the ultimate play.
In each glint and shine, let the smiles collide,
Creating a tapestry where laughter can hide.

Glistening Echoes in Silence

In a drawer full of clutter, it jostles,
A shiny friend with unexpected hustles.
When folks look closely, it winks with glee,
"Catch me if you can!" it taunts with esprit.

With a flick of the light, it dances around,
Causing bursts of laughter, joy unbound.
Who knew a little gem could steal the day,
With shimmer and charm, it leads all astray?

It rolls with the punches, never would frown,
Turning mundane moments to a festive crown.
A twirl, a swirl, in social grace,
Cheeky and bright, a true shining face!

At gatherings grand, it easily shines,
Woes turn to giggles as humor aligns.
So tip your glass to this playful tease,
For life's much more fun with a hint of cheese!

The Watchful Adornment

Perched on a lapel, it's eyes wide and keen,
This charming pin has seen it all, I mean!
Watching the gossip unfold with flair,
Not a single secret escapes its stare.

At the office, it giggles at HR's speech,
As it whispers, 'Don't take that route to breach!'
In the cafe, it mocks the coffee spill,
'Oh dear, more drama, is that a new thrill?'

It's a knowing ally, a mischievous mate,
Spreading joy in a most stylish state.
In meetings, it winks at the wildest of tales,
Prompting laughs that bravely set sails!

Once an unnoticed piece, how you've grown,
With laughter in corners you've brightly shone.
So here's to the smiles and chatter galore,
With you on my side, who could ask for more?

Stories Woven in Silver

In gleaming threads, a story alights,
Crafted with mischief, it playfully invites.
A zany history in delicate form,
Each twist and turn keeps its charm warm.

From a picnic mishap to dance floor frays,
It giggles at stories that stretch for days.
Remember that time when the cake took a dive?
It sparkled with mirth, oh how we survived!

With each subtle shift, it captures a gaze,
As it spreads delight in the silliest ways.
An artist of laughter, a muse of the proud,
It shimmers with secrets, never too loud.

So here's to the tales that it brings to light,
Of mishaps and giggles that feel just right.
In silver and style, we gather and cheer,
For life's a grand party with everyone near!

Radiance of the Unseen

Hiding in corners, it chuckles away,
A beacon of laughter in the light of day.
With secrets aplenty tucked under its shine,
It whispers, 'Join the fun, your turn to dine!'

As folks gather round, it slyly observes,
Turning simple moments to wild verve.
From tales of lost socks to the food fight's spree,
It glimmers with joy, a playful decree!

So dear little pin, you mischievous gem,
How splendid you make the mundane ahem!
With every chuckle that springs from your spark,
You unveil the beauty hidden in the dark.

As laughter breaches walls, it sets us all free,
In your radiant presence, we dance with glee.
For in nooks and crannies, joy needs to roam,
A hidden delight that always feels home!

www.ingramcontent.com/pod-product-compliance
Lightning Source LLC
Chambersburg PA
CBHW051732290426
43661CB00122B/239